VIRTUE AND HAPPINESS

THE MANUAL OF
EPICTETUS

CALLIGRAPHY BY
CLAUDE MEDIAVILLA

SHAMBHALA
Boston & London
2003

Shambhala Publications, Inc.
Horticultural Hall
300 Massachusetts Avenue
Boston, Massachusetts 02115
www.shambhala.com

English translation by Sherab Chödzin Kohn
Collection directed by Jean Mouttapa and Valérie Menanteau
Photography by Sylvie Durand

9 8 7 6 5 4 3 2 1

First Shambhala Edition
Printed in France by Pollina. L 88 312

⊖ This edition is printed on acid-free paper that meets the American
National Standards Institute z39.48 Standard.

Distributed in the United States by Random House, Inc.,
and in Canada by Random House of Canada Ltd

LIBRARY OF CONGRESS CATALOGING-IN-PUBLICATION DATA

Epictetus.
[Manual. English]
Virtue and Happiness: the manual of Epictetus/calligraphy by
Claude Mediavilla.—1st ed.
p. cm. — (Shambhala calligraphy)
Calligraphy in Greek.
ISBN 1-59030-052-1
1. Ethics. 2. Conduct of life. I. Mediavella, Claude. II. Title.
III. Series

B561.M52 E5 2003
188—dc21   2002011764

J UST THE NAME *Stoicism* by itself is enough call up in our minds the greatest school of moral philosophy of antiquity. It comes from the Greek *stoa*, which means "portico" and refers to the place where the disciples of Zeno of Citium (322–264 BCE) gathered. Far from any sort of speculative thought, this doctrine is built entirely around man, his destiny, and his happiness. This guiding idea pervades the entire history of this philosophical school, from the ancient Stoicism, represented by Zeno and Chrysippus, to that of the imperial Roman period, with which three names are associated: Seneca, Epictetus, and Marcus Aurelius.

History has preserved only a few elements of the life of Epictetus. He was born around 50 CE at Hierapolis in Phrygia and was for a long time the slave of Epaphroditus, himself a freed slave of Nero's. This person, whose name, even, is unknown to us—for Epictetus, which means "slave," is only an epithet—nevertheless found in his captivity the leisure time to study the lessons of a reputed philosopher, Musonius Rufus, who initiated him into the principles of the Stoic doctrine.

Having regained his freedom, Epictetus devoted himself entirely to philosophy. Driven by a desire to direct men's minds to the good, he taught Stoicism in Rome in spite of an imperial power that had little use for those pursuing the profession of philosophy. Rome by this time had long since supplanted Athens, and the empire was already undergoing a process of slow decomposition, marked by conspiracies and assassinations. Toward 94 CE, a decree by Domitian banished all philosophers from the city, qualifying them as enemies of the state. Driven from Italy, Epictetus took refuge in Nicopolis in Epirus. His teaching, which had been spurned up to this point, now met with great success. Epictetus made use by turns in his teaching of discourse, homily, interrogation, and commentary, displaying great subtlety in his mastery of the art of speech. He transmitted his knowledge orally, communicating to his students not only principles of philosophy but especially practical advice for living.

After his death, between 125 and 130, Flavius Arrian, who had followed Epictetus's courses, wrote up his notes in Greek, the cultivated language of the period, and published them in eight books, of which four are known to us under the title *Discourses*. Arrian also created a small work drawn from the discourses that contains the principal ideas of his master. This work is entitled *Enchiridion* in Greek, a term accurately translated as "Handbook," which is composed of fifty-three chapters. The *Handbook*, however, is not a synopsis of the Stoic doctrine, for it deals neither with the physics nor the logic. The purpose of the *Handbook* is a limited one; it is devoted to a single branch of Stoicism, its moral philosophy.

Conceived of as a small treatise of wisdom for the use of everyone, it does not follow a linear order. Different themes are dealt with in it: judgment, duty, action within the city or body politic, the will, exemplary behavior, choice, dignity, and so on. Twenty-four passages from the *Handbook* are presented here, excerpted from the translation, slightly revised, of François Thurot (nineteenth century). The reader is invited to wander through the pages at will and (re)discover the Stoic precepts, maxims for life worthy of meditation, which are based on the distinction between "that which depends upon us" and "that which does not depend upon us." The contemplation of this distinction is the first philosophical act to which Epictetus, as a guide of conscience, invites us. Understanding this will allow us to discern true values and to make proper use of our faculty of judgment.

Pascal said of Epictetus that, "among the philosophers of the world he was the one who knew best the duties of man." This was Pascal's homage to a great mind fully persuaded of the grandeur of humanity.

ΤῶΝ·ὌΝΤῶΝ·ΤΑ
ΜΕΝ·ἘΣΤΙΝ·ἘΦ
ἩΜῖΝ ΤΑ ΔΕ·ΟΥ
Κ·ἘΦ·ἩΜῖΝ·ἘΦ
ἩΜῖΝ·ΜΕΝ·Υ
ΠΟΛΗΥΙΣ·ΟΡΜ
Η·ὉΔΕΞΙΣ·ἜΚΚΛ
ΙΣΙΣ ΚΑΙ·ἘΝΙ·ΛΟ
Γῶ·ὍΣΑ·ἩΜΕΤΕ
ΡΑ·ἜΡΓΑ·ΟΥΚ·ἘΦ
ἩΜῖΝ·ΔΕ·ΤΟ·Σῶ

There is that which depends on us,
there is that which does not depend on us.
What depends on us
are our judgments,
our tendencies,
our desires,
our aversions—
in a word, everything that is
an action of our soul.
What does not depend on us
are our body,
fortune,
respectful opinions,
public appointments—
in a word, everything that is not
an action of our soul.

That which depends on us is
by nature, free,
without hindrance,
without conflict.
That which does not depend on us
is inconsistent, enslaved,
subject to hindrance, alien.

ΚΑΙ ΤΑ
ΜΕΝ ΕΦ ΗΜΙΝ
ΕΣΤΙ ΟΥΣΕΙ
ΕΛΕΥΘΕΡΑ·
ΑΚΩΛΥΤΑ
ΑΠΑΡΑΠΟΔΙΣΤΑ
ΤΑ ΔΕ ΟΥΚ
ΕΦ ΗΜΙΝ
ΑΣΘΕΝΗ
ΔΟΥΛΑ·

What troubles men
are not things,
but rather the judgments
they make about things.
For example, death has nothing about it
to be feared, or else
it would have appeared fearful to Socrates.
But the judgment that death has
something fearful about it—
that is what is fearful.

Ο ΘΑΝΑΤΟΣ
ΟΥΔΕΝ ΔΕΙΝ
ΟΝ, ΕΠΕΙ ΚΑΙ
ΣΩΚΡΑΤΕΙΑ
Ν ΕΦΑΙΝΕΤ
Ο · ΑΛΛΑ ΤΟ · Δ
ΟΓΜΑ · ΤΟ · ΠΕ
ΡΙ ΤΟΥ · ΘΑΝ
ΑΤΟΥ · ΔΙΟΤΙ
ΔΕΙΝΟΝ, ΕΚ
ΕΙΝΟ, ΤΟ · ΔΕΙ
ΝΟΝ · ΕΣΤΙΝ

Τὰ ἑαυτῶν
Δόγματα

When we are thwarted,
troubled, or aggrieved,
we should never blame anyone else
for this but ourselves,
that is, our own judgments.

Do not boast of any advantage
that belongs to someone else.
If a horse said with pride,
"I am beautiful,"
this would be tolerable;
but you, when you say with pride,
"I have a beautiful horse,"
know that you are boasting
of an advantage that belongs to the horse.
What then is yours?
The use you make of your ideas.

ὅταν λέγῃς
ἐπαιρόμενος ὅτι
Ἵππον καλὸν ἔχω,
ἴσθι ὅτι ἐπὶ ἵππου
ἀγαθῷ ἐπαίρῃ·
Τί οὖν ἐστι σόν;
Χρῆσις φαντασιῶν·

Ἀλλὰ
θέλε
Τὰ
γινόμενκ
ὡς
γίνεται,
καὶ
ευροηθεις

Do not ask for what happens
to happen as you desire it;
rather desire that things should happen
as they happen,
and you will be happy.

Remember that you should behave
in life as at a banquet.
The dish that is being passed around comes to you;
reach out your hand and take with discretion.
It is passed on: do not hold it back.
It has not yet arrived:
do not anticipate it from afar with your desires,
wait until it reaches you.
Do the same with children
with a woman, with public responsibilities,
with money, and you will be worthy to sit
one day at the table of the gods.
But if you do not take any of what is offered to you,
if you regard it with disdain,
then not only will you be a guest of the gods,
you will be their companion.
It was by behaving thus that Diogenes,
Heraclitus, and those who resemble them
became worthy of being called divine men.

Ἡράκλειτος

Διόδοτης

Remember that you are an actor
of a role that the author wanted a certain way:
short, if he wanted it short;
long, if he wanted it long.
If he wanted you to play the role
of a beggar, play it with talent;
the same for the role of a cripple,
an official, a simple private person.
It is up to you to play well
the character that is given to you.
But choosing it—
that is up to someone else.

Μέμνηƨο
ὅτι
ὑποκριτὴς
εἶ δράματος,
οἵον
ἂν θέλῃ ὁ
διδά-
καλος·

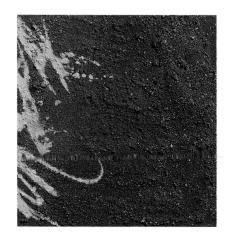

If you desire to be a philosopher,
expect from that moment
to be an object of derision, to be the butt
of mockery from a crowd of people who say:
"Suddenly he has come back to us a philosopher!"
and, "Where does his air of arrogance come from?"
Do not assume an arrogant air, but hold to that
which seems to you the best, with the conviction
that the divinity has assigned you to this post.
Remember that if you remain faithful to your principles,
those who mock you at first will admire you later on.
But if you are vanquished by their remarks,
you will make yourself ridiculous twice.

Εἰ φιλοσοφίας
ἐπιθυμεῖς,
παρασκ[ε]υάζου
αὐτόθεν
ὡς καταγελασ
θησόμενος

Ἀνίκητος
εἶναι
δύνασθαι
ἐὰν εἰς
μηδένα
ἄγονα
καταβαί
νης
ὁ ὄ οὐκ·

You can be invincible
If you do not engage
in any struggle
in which it does not depend on you
to be the winner.

"What place will I have in the City?"
The one you can have by remaining
a loyal and reserved man.
But if, in order to come to the aid of
your country, you lose these qualities,
what use can you be to it
having become impudent and disloyal?

ΟΥΛΑΤΤΩΝ
ἄμα
ΤΟΥ πιϭΤΟΝ
και
αἰδημονα

If your body were handed over
to the first comer
you would be indignant;
and you, when you hand over
your soul to the first comer
because he troubles it
and upsets it
with wounding remarks,
are you not ashamed?

Τὸ σῶμά
την,
γνώμην

First examine what it is
to be a philosopher;
then study your own nature
to see if you are up to it.
You want to be an athlete or
a wrestler?
Consider your arms, your thighs,
examine your loins.
One is endowed for one thing,
another for another.

την σεαυτου
φυσιν καταμαθε
ει δυνασαι
βαστασαι

Determine for yourself as of now
a way of life,
a plan of conduct
that you will follow,
both when you are alone
and when you find yourself
with others.

Most often, remain silent.
Or else only say
what is necessary, and in few words.

Μὴ ἀ1
πρὸ
λεχ9

If someone has just told you
that so-and-so is saying something bad about you,
do not try to justify yourself in the least
with regard to what has been reported to you;
only answer:
"He must not be fully informed
about all the other things that
could be said about me; otherwise
he would not have limited himself to that."

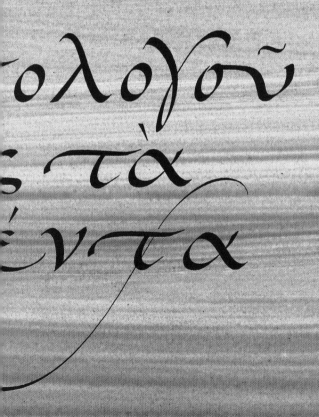

When an idea of pleasure
arises in your mind,
treat it like the others,
take care not to let yourself be carried away,
defer action, and obtain
from yourself some delay.

ἀλλ᾽
ἐκδεξάσθω
δὲ τὸ
πρᾶγμα

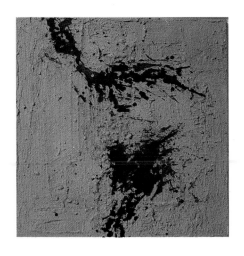

When you do something
after having recognized that it is
necessary to do it,
do not fear being seen doing it,
even if the crowd must
judge it unfavorably.
If you are wrong to do it,
avoid the action itself;
if you are right, why do you fear
those who will be wrong to blame you?

Εἰ δὲ
ὀρθῶς, τι
φοβῆ τοὺς
ἐπιπλήξοντας
οὐκ ὀρθῶς

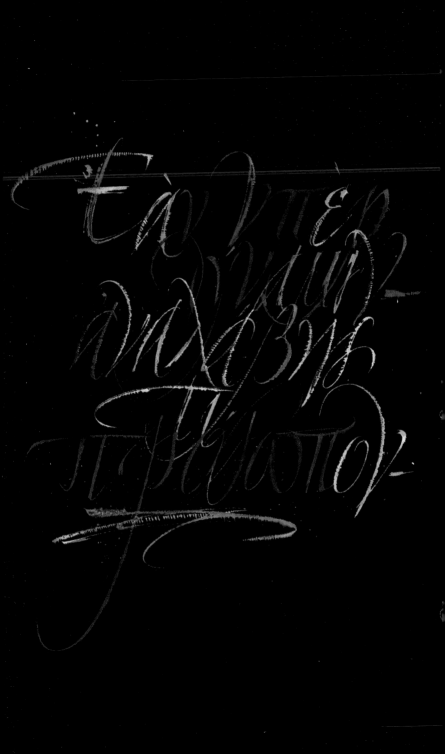

When you assume a role
that is beyond your powers,
not only will you cut a sorry figure at it,
but in addition you will have left aside
the role you could have fulfilled.

Once one has lost
the sense of measure,
there is no longer any limit.

As to the conduct and character of he
who is not a philosopher:
he does not look for profit
or for damage from himself
but rather from the outside.
As to the conduct and character
of a philosopher: he looks for
profit or for damage
only from himself.

φιλοδόξου
στάσις καὶ χαρακτὴρ
πᾶσαν ὠφέλειαν
καὶ βλάβην
ἐξ ἑαυτοῦ
προσδοκᾷ

Signs of someone who is progressing:
he blames no one,
he praises no one,
he complains of no one,
he accuses no one,
he never speaks of himself
as of someone important
or who knows something.

Σωκράτης

Socrates became what he was
because in every encounter,
he paid attention only to reason.
As for you, if you are not
yet Socrates, you should live as though
you wanted to be Socrates.

Ὅτι

τις πε

ἐπι ὁ

Τοῦτο γα

ἐστ

ὲ ἐρὲ

ρὶ ὁσῦ μὴ

ρέφρμ·

ρ οὐκ ἔτ

ὁόν·

No matter what they say about you,
do not be upset about it;
it no longer depends on you.

CLAUDE MEDIAVILLA

AS FAR BACK AS I CAN REMEMBER, the plastic arts always held a particular fascination for me. In a certain way, my destiny was already marked out from a very early age.

After my years of study at the Academy of Fine Arts in Paris, from which I received a degree, I enrolled in the Scriptorium de Toulouse, an advanced institute that provided instruction that was unique in France at that time. I had the opportunity for several years to give free rein to my passion for the sign and to try to find the beginnings of answers to the questions that were tormenting me because I sensed their importance for my future artistic choices. At the same time, I studied typography and took courses in paleography and the history of art at the faculty of letters. The excel-

lence of our calligraphy professor, the openness of his mind, the initiation he gave us into the calligraphies of Hebrew, Arabic, Chinese, and Greek, all counted for a great deal in shaping my mind, my vision of art in general, and my intuition.

Great importance is given in an apprenticeship in calligraphy to copying exercises, and also to analysis. An apprentice goes through pages and pages in his effort to understand a single letter. Then he needs pages and pages more to gain a glimpse of the spirit of a letter. For calligraphy, as the Greek etymology of the word—composed of the words *kallos* and *graphein*—tells us, is an art that has to do both with the beautiful and the good. To grasp the spirit of a letter is to see the truth and the self-evidence of lines and colors, and this definition holds for any style of writing, whatever its origin.

Because I was not confined to Latin calligraphy, I was able to experiment according to my whim and to experience for myself the forms created by artists belonging to cultures different from our own. In this way, I found points of agreement, affinities, oppositions or antinomies, but at the end of my exploration, the common creative elements that could be regarded as constants proved to be much more numerous than one might imagine. The main effect of this discovery was to permit me not to fall into the trap of exoticism, which tries to convince us that the more distant and incomprehensible a civilization seems, the greater its attraction.

After going through some professional experiences in various different societies, in 1975 I opened my own creative studio in Paris. This was an exciting adventure that gave me the opportunity to encounter an expanded clientele, often international, and to come up with original solutions to specific creative problems. Very quickly, I was receiving orders from important personalities. Official organizations, the office of the presidency of France, editors, public relations firms, and industries charged me with different tasks, as for example, engraving inscriptions on the royal tombs in the Basilica of Saint-Denis, a work commissioned in 1993 by the Minister of Culture for the bicentennial of the death of Louis XVI.

Starting in the 1980s, I began to distance myself from the figurative painting I had been working on since childhood, because it left me feeling unsatisfied. At the same time, I no longer wanted to limit myself to traditional calligraphy, whether Arabic, Latin, or any other. And even though attaining this goal was already very difficult, I wished to follow a different path, the path of personal expression. I glimpsed vast possibilities for calligraphy, but I also felt I had to apply this art in a new way. This gave me an especially good reason to return to my first love, painting, and enabled me to take my creative effort a step further.

The project I undertook in relation to the present volume fit in perfectly with this new direction. My interest in the Greek script is related primarily to the cursive form of these letters, which moreover is close to that of the Arabic script. There are very surprising common features between Greek and Arabic, which I have tried to highlight in several of my calligraphies. The fact that the Greeks created the first alphabet, even if their invention was based on the Phoenician system, was also a key element in my decision to calligraph certain passages from the *Handbook* of Epictetus. Especially by introducing vowels into the alphabet, the Greeks rationalized writing and took to its most extreme degree of abstraction. On account of this essential point, I feel a very close affinity with Greek, since my work in calligraphy and in painting is based entirely on this idea of abstraction. What is calligraphy really if not the artistic discipline whose object is to depict abstract signs? And if this art of lines and marks touches the very heart of the onlooker, is this not precisely because, in contrast to figurative works, it depends on no discourse, no story line? And this is the source of my principal concern in my compositions: not just to create a link between calligraphy and painting but to reconcile them well and truly, to bring them into harmony with each other.

For this edition, I used pens for the lines and flat brushes for the colors. The small bottles of tinctures of indigo and curcuma (turmeric) [depicted in the illustration] date from 1870 and are representative of my preferences with regard to color. Curcuma is a root used in Asia to produce an orangish-yellow tincture. Indigo is a pigment from which a variety of different blues can be made, even a very dark blue. I have always been attracted to the tones of ochre, which I put together with blues or reds that intervene and break the rhythm or even upset the harmony of a composition. Thus my work leads me to use colors that I characterize as "dangerous," like the green or the pink that can be seen through my pigment jars below. I am convinced that a certain form of insolence, such as the utilization of fluorescent colors, must have its place in the work of art. However, this particular insolence, which surprises and amazes us, requires a special apprenticeship of its own; it requires a perfectly mastered technique all to itself. It is only on this condition that it is possible for it to be neither excessive nor vulgar, but truly artistic. The counterpoise generated by these so-called dangerous colors brings force and

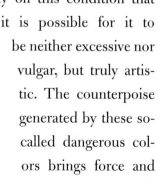

power to a work. It then becomes the entire task of the calligrapher or painter to modulate the colors to wed them better.

As for the lines themselves, they obey precise typographical and esthetic rules, yet still leave room for personal expression in their composition. From uppercase Greek to the several cursive forms of the script, from the uncial with its very round proportions, through the Greek of the Renaissance, up to the most modern form of Greek, which is very close to complete abstraction, I have offered a spectrum of the different styles so as to provide a glimpse of the range of possible graphic creation within them. But only rigorous mastery of the formal, technical elements makes it possible to grasp the purity of the letters, beyond their meaning in the conventional language. The gesture of the calligrapher or abstract painter becomes the expression of truth when he captures the breath, the life that circulates in the forms.

Since the time I understood that calligraphy was linked with abstract painting, I have devoted myself body and soul to both of these disciplines, my most constant desire from that point on being to take abstract art to a high level by means of the self-evidence of the fullness of its forms and the expressive emotion that arises from its content and composition. The lines, the marks, the forms have an identity, a face and a soul that we are urgently called upon to sense and to master. It goes without saying that no one can penetrate without guidance and initiation this infinitely rich world. Indeed the mastery of the sign is a form of asceticism. Like the martial arts, it requires a total discipline of the right side of the brain, the side connected with the nonlinear, the spontaneous, the symbolic. Lightninglike illumination made fertile by the rigorous control mastered during one's apprenticeship are what make the work of art. This experience allowed me to appreciate better what I call "great art," to better understand its spirit and the genius that brings to life these creative configurations with surfaces bursting with light or humming with energy. It is only through a long-term exploration of the beings and things of the world that one can pretend to any such result. Freed of the obligation to represent and far from being limited to reproducing an external envelope, the artist who is nourished by the calligraphic tradition is in a position to produce living works in which an explosion of emotion takes place. The moment of becoming aware of the emotional dimension of the line is a decisive one for the very

manner in which an artist envisages his work. May this discovery, which contributes to the revelation of one of the unrecognized but fundamental aspects of abstract art, illuminate pictorial creation with a new light.

Claude Mediavilla

Mediavilla